Other Books by

"Ooh, look at these good and available books. You know which one was the best? . . . Both of them!"

A **TREASURY** OF COMICS BY

guy &
rOdd

Andrews McMeel
Publishing, LLC

Kansas City

Brevity is distributed by United Feature Syndicate, Inc.

Brevity Remix copyright © 2008 by Guy & Rodd. All rights reserved. Printed in China. No part of this book may be used or reproduced in any manner whatsoever without written permission except in the case of reprints in the context of reviews. For information, write Andrews McMeel Publishing, LLC, an Andrews McMeel Universal company, 4520 Main Street, Kansas City, Missouri 64111.

08 09 10 11 12 SDB 10 9 8 7 6 5 4 3 2 1

ISBN-13: 978-0-7407-7228-3
ISBN-10: 0-7407-7228-7

Library of Congress Control Number: 2007939268

www.andrewsmcmeel.com

───── **ATTENTION: SCHOOLS AND BUSINESSES** ─────

Andrews McMeel books are available at quantity discounts with bulk purchase for educational, business, or sales promotional use. For information, please write to: Special Sales Department, Andrews McMeel Publishing, LLC, 4520 Main Street, Kansas City, Missouri 64111.

Guy dedicates this book to Joanna, Rich, George, and all the folks in Ann Arbor who have been so nice and supportive . . . not to mention gorgeous.

 Rodd dedicates this book to Larry Page and Sergey Brin, the founders of Google, in the hope they will make guyandrodd.com the first result for the search term "new yorker cartoons." Not because we've ever had a cartoon published in the *New Yorker*, but, you know, just to piss them off.

Introduction

A lot of people have complained that our comics are too funny.

They are upset because of all the uncontrollable laughter our jokes inspire.

They constantly write us and ask if there's any way to tone down the guffaw factor.

Well, don't worry. We have heard your prayers and, like Zeus, we have answered them.

We have spent hours adding uninteresting, unfunny commentary in order to make this book academic and dull.

Now you can read these comics in peace. And without the painful rib sores that accompanied our first two books.

To make it easy to know whose inane notes you're reading, we've included visual representations of ourselves.

This is Guy: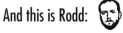

And this is Rodd:

In the print world, these icons are called dingbats. It seems like we should make a dumb joke here, but you'll find plenty of that brand of easy humor down the aisle from this book in the *Pearls Before Swine* treasury.

Thanks for making *Brevity* a part of your world. Feel free to drop us a line at guyandrodd@gmail.com to let us know how we're doing.

This was our first comic ever printed, and it's still most people's favorite. Which means, scientifically, it has been all downhill since the moment we began.

This is the first comic Rodd wrote, and it was our editor's favorite. Rodd got off to a strong start by writing 25 percent of the comics on this page . . . he has written five in the three years since then.

BEFORE BIRDS AND BEES

AFTER ALL THE SCORES WERE TABULATED, YOGI WOULD BE ASHAMED TO DISCOVER THAT HE WASN'T ACTUALLY SMARTER THAN THE AVERAGE BEAR, THAT HE WAS IN FACT STUPIDER... AND BY QUITE A LARGE MARGIN.

 Right about the time of this caption, it becomes painfully clear that brevity isn't actually one of our strong suits.

"I'M SORRY FRIEND, BEING ELVIS IS ALL IN THE HIPS AND, WELL, YOU KNOW..."

ONE DAY MIKE AND A HANDFUL OF OTHER TERMITES HAPPENED UPON A TURKEY SANDWICH... AFTER THAT IT WAS PRETTY HARD TO GO BACK TO WOOD.

First off, these are huge termites. Secondly, I do spend way too much time thinking about things like this. I mean, really, does a termite ever take a bite of something that's not made of wood, and just go "Whoa!"

"WAKE UP, KID. WE'VE GOT SOME PARTY GAMES OF OUR OWN WE'D LIKE TO PLAY."

In the original drawing of this, one of the donkeys has a human butt with a thumbtack through it. I can't remember if the syndicate made us take that out, or if we realized no one could tell what it was supposed to be, 'cause honestly, a butt separated from the rest of a person doesn't look like much. (I don't know this from personal experience or anything.)

LAZY.

13

Any professional artist will tell you the perspective here is all wrong. Even though I think I've become a better artist by doing this damn comic every day, I still don't think I could draw this correctly.

A competitor who does a harmless little comic strip had his syndicate send letters to all the newspapers claiming that we stole this idea from him. Of course that's not possible, because, like almost everyone in America, neither of us has ever read his strip.

This was the very beginning of my fascination with potatoes, the Cadillac of root vegetables.

NOBODY TOLD JAMES THAT THE FIVE SECOND RULE DIDN'T APPLY IN THEIR LINE OF WORK.

HE ONLY HAD ENOUGH MONEY FOR ONE, AND FOR THE LIFE OF HIM HE COULDN'T REMEMBER THE DIFFERENCE.

 I love the sales guy. He knows the answer, but isn't getting involved 'cause it's not his place to interfere.

"I'D ALWAYS HOPED THAT I'D LEAVE THIS MORTAL COIL SURROUNDED BY MY BEAUTIFUL, LOVING FAMILY... SO CAN SOME OF YOU UGLY ONES MOVE TO THE BACK?"

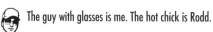 The guy with glasses is me. The hot chick is Rodd.

OH MY GOSH, THEY'RE EATING IT! THIS IS SOOOO GROSS! WAIT 'TIL I TELL THE GIRLS!

SIX DAYS LATER THEY WOULD CROSS PATHS WITH HURRICANE ISABELLE, AND DISCOVER THAT IT REALLY WASN'T SUCH A GOOD SHIP AFTER ALL.

This comic was scheduled to run right after the tsunami struck Thailand in 2004. It was rescheduled.

THE TOWN OF IRONY, PENNSYLVANIA HAS LONG BEEN KNOWN FOR BEING VERY LITERAL.

Three years later, and still no strip has generated more mail. Our editor calls this our "Cow Tools."

THROUGH YEARS OF COMPUTER ANALYSIS AND CRYPTOCARTOGRAPHY, WE ARE CONVINCED THIS IS THE SPOT WHERE THE 18TH CENTURY GALLEY "ARUBIDIS" WENT DOWN WITH HER PRECIOUS CARGO OF GOLD, SILVER, AND RUBBER DUCKIES... OF COURSE, ONLY TIME WILL TELL.

There is probably an actual word for the technique salvagers use to find things, but research is tough, and inventing words is a much better fit for my overall laziness.

 This comic made more sense in 2005, before Japan slid into the bottom ten of all countries on standardized tests.

UNBEKNOWNST TO MOST, DOGS ARE ACTUALLY GREEDY BASTARDS SEARCHING FOR GOLD.

 In newspapers this was changed to greedy devils . . . this book just got dangerous.

"I'M SORRY TIMMY, BUT IF I KEEP GOING FOR HELP, YOU'LL NEVER LEARN TO TAKE CARE OF YOURSELF."

THE NEXT FEW YEARS WOULD BE VERY LITIGIOUS.

YES, WELL, TECHNICALLY 47 *IS* A NEW RECORD. BUT MORE IMPORTANTLY, THIS IS A PIE-*MAKING* CONTEST.

 For some reason I was totally positive we needed to add "and you just ate all the entries" to the end of this caption. Luckily Rodd embarrassed me into taking that out.

WHY DO I ALWAYS ATTRACT THE UGLY ONES?

MIRROR, MIRROR, ON THE...

 Penguins are funny lookin'.

FIRST HE FELT PRIDE, THEN CONFUSION, THEN THE TERRIBLE DOUBTS BEGAN TO SEEP IN... HAD HE FORGOTTEN, ONCE AGAIN, TO TELL DARRYL THEY WERE GOING TO PLAY HIDE AND SEEK?

"THE LAST THING HE SAID WAS 'I'M GOING TO GO LOOK UP THE WORD "DICTIONARY" IN THE DICTIONARY', AND THEN THE UNIVERSE KIND OF COLLAPSED AROUND HIM."

 The guy in the background hasn't yet noticed that his little dog was just horribly crushed into oblivion. But don't worry . . . he was an evil dog who hated America.

HURRY UP, MAN, I CAN'T HOLD THIS FOREVER.

BEFORE THEY SETTLED ON WATER, SHOWER PIONEERS EXPERIMENTED WITH A NUMBER OF ALTERNATIVES, INCLUDING SPAGHETTI.

 I've always thought this should read "early" shower pioneers, even though I know that's redundant.

CONGRATULATIONS! IT'S A SPORK.

 What are those stirrups for?

...AND FOR YOU, THE SHINY OBJECT WITH A SIDE ORDER OF CRAYONS.

TODDLER RESTAURANTS

TO TELL YOU THE TRUTH, I'M NOT EVEN THAT HUNGRY... BUT WHEN I SEE THOSE MARBLES, I JUST LOSE IT.

"NO, I'M ACTUALLY THE *LONELY* RANGER, BUT IF YOU WANT TO TALK... YOU DON'T? OH."

EVER SINCE HE WAS A LITTLE MAGAZINE HE HAD BEEN DEATHLY AFRAID OF SPIDERS, AND HE DIDN'T LIKE WHERE THIS WAS GOING.

SUDDENLY JOHN REALIZED HE DIDN'T WANT PAPER <u>OR</u> PLASTIC. HE WANTED SOMETHING NEW... SOMETHING FANTASTIC.

 Rodd had to change John's expression a couple times . . . it kept looking like the fantastic new thing he wanted was the grocery bagger.

"I'M SORRY JAKE... I'M STARVING TO DEATH, MY HAIR'S A MESS, AND I JUST DON'T FEEL LIKE POSING ANYMORE."

 Jake was the editor who signed us. He's awesome, but now he works on real books with jillions of words and big ideas and crap like that.

21

 I think this is my favorite one ever.

Out of all the mean-spirited comics we've done, this one makes me cringe a little bit every time. Maybe it's because I have three ugly, ungrateful sons of my own.

The other option for this was both of them in a tow truck towing the other tow truck, and the passenger says, "No, Gerald, I'm not sure I do see the irony." But I think this way is probably better, and also we were still a little shell-shocked from our last adventure in "irony."

THEY WERE YOUNG AND IN LOVE, AND HAROLD
WOULD SPEND WHOLE WEEKENDS COUNTING THE
FRECKLES ON ARLENE'S BACK. OF COURSE THEY
WERE ALSO INCREDIBLY STUPID...
ARLENE ONLY HAD SEVEN FRECKLES.

The syndicate made Rodd draw a bathing suit on her, even though you couldn't see anything in the original drawing.

JERRY KEPT ALL OF HIS PRESS CLIPPINGS IN A SCRAPBOOK.

...AND HERE'S MY NAME ON THE COVER OF NEWSWEEK.

Newsweek

THUK!

NEWTON DISCOVERS ANTI-GRAVITY

THE VILLAGE OF THE DARNED

OOH, I STUBBED MY TOE!

I CAN'T HEAR YOU, I'VE GOT A CHICKEN IN MY EAR!

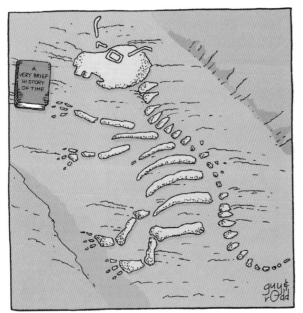

ON A HOT DAY IN 1941, SCIENTISTS UNCOVERED THE ONLY KNOWN REMAINS OF THE ELUSIVE NERDOSAURUS REX.

Occasionally I'll draw a detail that needs an extra caption, like the book this skeleton is holding. Sometimes I'll wing it and write it myself, but in this case, Guy's was much better than mine.

IT TURNS OUT THEY DON'T GO TOGETHER SO WELL.

CAUTION! DO NOT TOUCH! EXTREME DANGER OF ELECTRICAL SHOCK!!!

Rodd put a message in the braille that says, "Guy loves Sarah Silverman." I didn't realize this until the *San Francisco Chronicle* reported on it. My girlfriend didn't realize it until whatever time it is when she gets to this page.

"OH, SO WHEN YOU SAID YOU WERE AN EXOTIC DANCER YOU MEANT, WELL...EXOTIC."

 This really happens. Possibly. I don't know. But it would make sense if it did. Again, research is tough.

 This actually did happen. I researched it and everything.

HEY, WE'RE ONE MAN SHORT OF A HORDE... WHATCHA DOIN' TODAY?

FOR ONE EMBARRASSING WEEK, HEAVEN RAN OUT OF NORMAL WINGS.

SLOWLY, ALMOST IMPERCEPTIBLY, FEELINGS OF FUTILITY STARTED TO CREEP IN.

I don't actually have anything to say about these three comics, but the page looked really blank. I like that shirt you are wearing right now.

I can't believe this one got by the censors.

 Seriously, you look great. And you have really good taste in books. But even if you didn't, your looks would be enough to carry you through.

EARLY TREADMILLS

BILL'S CLOTHES CLASH

I went through a whole phase where I made T-shirts that said stupid things like "Hasselhoff," "apathy!," "eagle rock: this bird knows how to party," and the one pictured here, "Vilanch." Weirdly, Bruce Vilanch never responded to this.

FOR SEVERAL MINUTES, NORMA'S BODY IS
POSSESSED BY THE SPIRIT OF HER
DEAD WASHING MACHINE.

"MAYBE I SHOULDN'T HAVE
BROUGHT THE TERMITES"

"THE PROFILE SAYS OUR SUSPECT IS
SOMETHING OF A LADIES' MAN...
YOU'RE FREE TO GO."

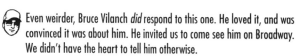 Even weirder, Bruce Vilanch *did* respond to this one. He loved it, and was
convinced it was about him. He invited us to come see him on Broadway.
We didn't have the heart to tell him otherwise.

In our first book, this comic was printed in black and white, so it made no sense. I know what you're thinking: it still doesn't.

STUPID HAMSTER.

In addition to dressing well, and having a good sense of humor, people like you because you have a pleasant smell.

CENSUS

"FOUR MILLION, EIGHT HUNDRED SEVENTEEN THOUSAND SIXTY THREE ... TWO? WAIT... FOUR ... WAIT, OH BOY, I PROBABLY SHOULD HAVE BEEN WRITING THIS DOWN."

"NOW THAT YOU'RE 10, WE CAN TELL YOU THE TRUTH: BEAUTY ISN'T ACTUALLY IN THE EYE OF THE BEHOLDER, THERE ARE INTERNATIONAL STANDARDS... AND YOU HAVEN'T MET THEM."

"...A RACCOON, SURE, EVEN A SKUNK WOULD BE OK, BUT THE CAT?!"

We got kicked out of about a dozen papers for this, and got tons of angry e-mails from offended citizenry. Apparently everyone thinks you can see the dog's wang, even though Rodd insists that's just a piece of hay. Also, in our defense, animals don't do it that way . . . at least not when I'm watching.

ACTUALLY, I'M A NERDIVORE. I ONLY EAT YOUR LAMER PLANTS AND ANIMALS: DUCKBILL PLATYPI, CUMQUATS, DAFFODILS, THE OCCASIONAL MUDSHARK.

This is the first in my "Bill Cosby sweater" phase. I thought if I threw these awful fashion items on our unsuspecting characters, they would appear even more ridiculous. Interestingly, the only place you can find these sweaters today are in big and tall catalogs. You may not have known that, but I am 6'8", and painfully aware of how the world views men like me.

FREAK

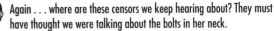
Again . . . where are these censors we keep hearing about? They must have thought we were talking about the bolts in her neck.

What, in the name of all that is holy, is the deal with clamato? It's clam liquid and tomato juice, and one of those things should never be an ingredient in any kind of drink. I mean, honestly, tomato juice!? Barf.

"LOOK AT THAT PLUMAGE.
HE MUST BE THE ALPHA MALE."

MY CHILD IS AN HONOR STUDENT AT
GLASSLICKER ELEMENTARY SCHOOL

The number one question I get asked is, "Where do your ideas come from?" I generally answer, "My brain." But on this one, I just don't know.

My wife has this bumper sticker on her minivan. OK, I put it there.

FOR EONS SHE LULLED US INTO COMPLACENCY WITH HER WHOLE ORBITING SATELLITE SHTICK... THEN, WHEN WE LEAST EXPECTED IT, THE MOON ATTACKED.

MYSELF, I'M A KILLER BEE...
SO WHAT ARE YOU, A ZOMBIE BEE,
TORMENT BEE, DISEASE BEE...
DON'T TELL ME YOU'RE A HONEY BEE?
OH DEAR GOD, A HONEY BEE!?

Keen-eyed readers will note the debut of the computerized font version of my own handwriting. Before that, every individual letter was drawn by hand. As if Guy's captions are worth that kind of effort.

SURE, THEY WERE ONLY NICKELS, BUT THE IMPORTANT THING IS THAT ADULTS EVERYWHERE FELT STUPID.

THE DEADLY NINJA CLOWNS OF GUANGZHOU PROVINCE

 Ninjas don't live in Guangzhou. Thank you, five ninja nerds who pointed that out. Like I said, research makes my brain hurt.

WATCH OUT, THAT SQUIRREL'S ABOUT TO STEAL YOUR CRUMBS!

Another loser fashion item: the coordinated tracksuit. I wore one of these in gym class in seventh grade (green with black stripes).

GEE, NO HAROLD, I DIDN'T CHECK THE ONE PLACE ON MY BODY WHERE I CAN STORE THINGS. THANK GOODNESS I'VE GOT A GENIUS LIKE YOU AROUND TO POINT OUT THE TOTALLY OBVIOUS THINGS THAT... OH WAIT, THERE THEY ARE.

This probably happens to kangaroos more often than you think. Not with keys, 'cause they don't use them, but random things like a berry that they find a week later and were like, oh, I was wondering what happened to that. (Do kangaroos eat berries? I refuse to look it up.)

WOW, THEY LOOK JUST A TINY BIT SMALLER FROM UP HERE

Again with the perspective! I thought cartoonery was supposed to be easy, which is why *Dilbert* looks like a child drew it.

"YOU'RE THE GREATEST CAN I'VE EVER MET. I JUST KNOW WE'LL GROW OLD TOGETHER ON THIS FENCE POST!"

"IT'S EITHER A BOO-BOO OR AN OWWIE, BUT THE DOCTORS NEED TO RUN SOME MORE TESTS BEFORE THEY DECIDE."

"NAH, I WASN'T REALLY AFRAID. SEE, EVEN THOUGH HE'S PRETTY MIGHTY AS FAR AS MICE GO, HE'S STILL, WELL, A MOUSE."

Guy wanted Mighty Mouse to be lying in a pool of blood, but I couldn't bring myself to do it for some reason.

"I ASSURE YOU MADAM, THAT THE UGLIFICATION FACTOR OF THIS MIRROR IS NO GREATER THAN THE NATIONALLY ACCEPTED ONE-TO-ONE STANDARD."

MAN, YOU REALLY LOOK GREAT TODAY, HOUSE.

AH, SHUCKS GUY, I'M JUST A REGULAR OLD HOUSE.

MY HUMBLE ABODE

That's my actual car, but not my actual house. Rodd knows my car because we used to work together, but he has no idea what my house looks like because I have never invited him over. (For the record, my house looks like a mansion!)

meta

15 BILLION DOLLARS LATER, THEY DISCOVERED, TO THEIR EMBARRASSMENT, THAT THERE WAS ACTUALLY NO PRACTICAL APPLICATION FOR AN UNSTEALTH BOMBER.

"AMBROSIA AND NECTAR AGAIN. WHAT I WOULDN'T GIVE FOR SOME TAP WATER RIGHT NOW."

WON-TON DISREGARD FOR THE LAW

Rodd thought this was stupid, and didn't want to do it. I would like to take this opportunity to apologize to him. Rodd, I'm sorry; you were right.

Those prunes could probably still score with the plums, 'cause look how much richer they are.

WHILE SINGING THE POPULAR SONG, CLAY WAS DISTURBED TO DISCOVER THAT HIS THIGH BONE WASN'T CONNECTED TO HIS HIP BONE, THAT IT WAS, IN FACT, CONNECTED TO NOTHING.

YOUNG GREG DISCOVERS IN THE SAME DAY THAT HE IS A HOMO SAPIEN AND HIS EPIDERMIS IS SHOWING.

"'LA PRESIDENCIA', 'PALAIS DU GENERAL', BUT NO, YOU HAD TO LET YOUR IDIOT BROTHER EARL NAME THE HOUSE."

"Human Desire"
by Hiyam Miyuki
medium: bricks, mortar, bucket

This is not a real well, it is an analogy for the unobtainable, the dream, the impossible dream that makes life so challenging yet so rewarding.

I hope you like it!

This guy probably isn't the first to die from modern art. "Miyuki" was a shout-out to another cartoonist who was on Comics Sherpa at the same time as us. I forget her first name. I refuse to research it.

Jennifer Miyuki Babcock.

DYSLEXICS ARE THE LEADING CAUSE OF
TRAFFIC JAMS AT KITCHEN STORES.

 We got some hate mail over this one. Probably I should have seen it
coming, but I didn't think they'd be able to read the strip in the first place.

"...AND WE'LL JUST FOLLOW THE BREAD
CRUMBS OUT OF THE FOREST, AND...
OH JEEZ, I'M AN IDIOT"

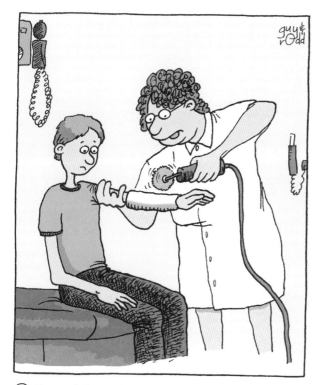

 This actually happened to me. I swear. I've only had a cast once, and the
woman who cut it off was missing a finger. I was twelve, and terrified.

 Way to give the joke away, jerk. People usually stare at this thing all
day trying to figure it out.

"EXCUSE ME, BUT WHICH AISLE
DID YOU FIND THOSE ON?"

 Every time we draw a witch we try to have her say "which."

41

This was a particularly pleasant image for little kids on Sunday morning.

"SO YOU JUST DRY STUFF? THAT'S COOL, I GUESS. I MEAN, IT'S NOT LIKE THERE'S SOME MYSTICAL FORCE THAT COULD DO THAT FOR YOU, LIKE, I DON'T KNOW... EVAPORATION."

"SO ANYWAYS, IF YOU'RE NOT DOING ANYTHING LATER MAYBE WE COULD GO BACK TO MY PLACE AND I COULD, SHALL WE SAY, TAKE A FEW LIBERTIES WITH YOU."

It must be tough being one of those hideous monsters. You're almost always the only one of your kind . . . Godzilla, King Kong, Dr. Phil, etc.

I CAN TOTALLY DRAW BETTER THAN THIS.

Should probably be "that" not "this," right?

THE GUINNESS BOOK OF MUNDANE ACHIEVEMENTS WAS A MUCH SLOWER SELLER.

IDENTICAL TWINS ARE SLIGHTLY OVERWEIGHT.

MAN EATS 3 HOT DOGS AT PICNIC.

See if you can find the twins in another comic. There are many instances of stealing artwork from myself in this book. E-mail us if you think you've found them all. There are also a few other shout-outs to famous people who probably don't need any help from us, like Tenacious D.

When we were young and posting comics on the Internet, we didn't use lame, PG-rated phrases like "screw up." I'm just sayin' . . . you know, we were pretty hardcore.

Lots of people didn't get this. If you are among them, making a huge diamond look like a huge piece of gold actually makes it look less valuable.

Ohhhh!

AT THE CAMEL-DROMEDARY PEACE TALKS.

"ONE HUMP, TWO HUMPS, WHAT DOES IT MATTER?
THE POINT IS ... WE'RE ALL FREAKS.
OH GOD, I WISH I WAS A HORSE."

 I thought I was pretty clever coming up with a logo for some sort of imaginary camel/dromedary association, but looking at it now, it's the stupidest thing ever.

"OKAY GENTLEMEN, HITLER'S INVADED POLAND, THE JAPANESE HAVE ATTACKED PEARL HARBOR, ALL THE GREAT NATIONS OF THE WORLD ARE MOBILIZING FOR WAR. THIS IS GONNA BE BIG, FATTY ARBUCKLE BIG, BIGGER THAN WORLD WAR I EVEN, AND WE NEED A NAME THAT MAKES THAT CLEAR... SOMETHING CLEVER AND UNEXPECTED, SOMETHING NO ONE BUT A TOTAL GENIUS WOULD COME UP WITH."

A group of nerds online called this the biggest insult to intelligence of all time. Nerds.

PUBLICLY, GWEN WOULD PRETEND TO BE THRILLED, BUT THE TRUTH WAS THAT ALL SHE HAD REALLY WANTED TO DO WAS MAKE OUT WITH A TOAD.

It's not easy to get bestiality into the funny papers. I think we did a good job with this one.

AHH, CRUEL FATE. FOR YEARS WILBUR HAD DREAMED OF TASTING AN APPLE, BUT NOT LIKE THIS, NO NEVER LIKE THIS.

 Wilbur has a cameo in another comic. All right, I'm not giving away any more.

"YOU KNOW, I'M REALLY STARTING TO GET SICK OF CRUMBS. JUST ONCE I'D LIKE A FULL MEAL... WELL THOUGHT OUT, AND CAREFULLY PREPARED."

IT WASN'T THE FIRST BAD DECISION RON O'NEAL MADE, BUT IT WOULD BE THE LAST.

Ron O'Neal is one of the great salesmen at our syndicate. At some point we told him if he sold five new papers, we'd write him into a comic. I'm not sure how happy he was with his "prize" at the end of the day.

SUDDENLY, MARMADUKE DISCOVERED THAT
HIS WHOLE LIFE WAS A JOKE...
AND NOT A VERY FUNNY ONE EITHER.

We got some angry letters in defense of Brad Anderson. Rodd replied that we had Brad's blessing and he was going to do one about us in return, which totally shut everyone up. Of course, it wasn't true.

"SOON YOU WILL START TO NOTICE CHANGES TO YOUR BODY... MASSIVE, HORRIFYING CHANGES."

"IT'S A HATRED BRACELET.
I MADE IT FOR YOU."

"... AND I WOULD HAVE GOTTEN AWAY WITH IT TOO, IF IT WASN'T FOR THOSE DANG MEDDLING KIDS... THAT AND MY INCREDIBLY STUPID PLAN. ALSO, IN RETROSPECT, I REALIZE MY COSTUME WAS, REGRETTABLY, QUITE LAME."

Harold is about to jab that fork through his wife's soft pallet. Rodd has serious anger issues.

SHORTLY AFTER DISCOVERING THAT SOME OF THE LOWER PRIMATES ALSO USED TOOLS, AN EXPLORER IN ZAMBEZI DISCOVERED THEIR PATENT OFFICE.

PAtents

Patent no. 8
sorta use a rock to bang on a nut or something.

Lots of times, a couple months will go by, and I'll start to hate the wording in a joke, but not this time. We did this one two years ago, and I am still ridiculously proud of "patent 8."

HISTORY HAS LONG FORGOTTEN THE REST OF THE SPEECH.

"GIVE ME LIBERTY OR GIVE ME DEATH... OR CHICKS, YOUNG CHICKS WHO KNOW HOW TO HAVE A GOOD TIME. OR GADGETS, OR, LIKE, MONEY. OR A REALLY NICE COAT, BLUE MAYBE ..."

7-12

UH-OH

7-11 GUS

"YOU KNOW THERE WERE 7,184 WAVES YESTERDAY. THAT'S JUST SLIGHTLY MORE THAN USUAL. I THINK THAT'S ONE OF MY FAVORITE THINGS ABOUT ISLAND LIFE, THERE'S ALWAYS A SURPRISE AROUND THE CORNER. WHAT'S YOUR FAVORITE THING, ED?"

"WE'RE MUTINYING SIR. WE'RE SICK OF YOUR ATTITUDE, YOUR PUNISHMENTS ARE TOO HARSH, AND FRANKLY, WE'RE NOT EVEN SURE WHY WE NEED A CAPTAIN."

 Moments later they all died of asphyxiation.

"OH HIM, THAT'S MOSQUITO MAN ... HE'S ANNOYING ALRIGHT, BUT PRETTY HARMLESS AS FAR AS SUPER VILLAINS GO."

IN 1970, HAVING ASSUMED IT WAS A SCIENCE COMPETITION, STEPHEN HAWKING WAS DEVASTATED WHEN HE LOST THE TITLE OF "MR. UNIVERSE" TO A COMPLETE IDIOT.

 Arnold Schwarzenegger won the Mr. Universe competition in 1970, but he's not a complete idiot. That part is made up.

"HEY, DO WE EVEN NEED THESE TUNNELS? WHAT IF WE'RE JUST DOING THIS TO AMUSE THESE PEOPLE?"

Rodd and I both used to work at a company called the Ant Farm. Now he runs it. And he's totally full of himself.

EARLY ARCHAEOLOGY

"IT APPEARS TO BE SOME SORT OF BONE."

FOR YEARS HE HAD SPENT EVERY FREE MOMENT WORKING ON HIS PERPETUAL MOTION MACHINE. SO FAR, HE WAS UP TO 18 SECONDS.

For a woman who loves shopping so much, she really is dressed pretty plainly.

William Terwilliger was a professor of mine at Ithaca College. Not sure how he made it into the caption, since I didn't write it.

LATER THAT NIGHT, TIM CREPT INTO ANDY'S
CAVE AND COCONUTTED HIM TO DEATH.

Rodd came up with the verb *coconutted*, which is the best part of
this cartoon.

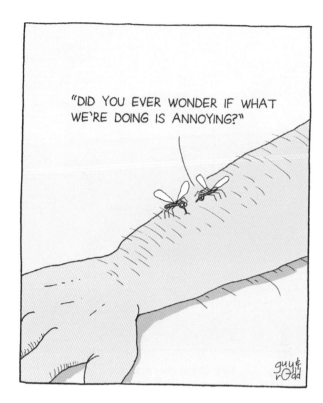

IN CASE THINGS HAD TURNED OUT DIFFERENTLY,
THE FRENCH WERE READY WITH AN EQUALLY
SPECTACULAR STATUE OF SHAME.

MOST PEOPLE DON'T KNOW THAT CATS AND
DOGS USED TO BE BEST FRIENDS UNTIL SOME
THOUGHTLESS CARTOONIST BEGAN STIRRING UP
TROUBLE IN SEARCH OF EASY GAGS.

EVENTUALLY THE ZEBRAS FIGURED OUT THAT THEY COULD AVOID DETECTION BY HANGING OUT IN FRONT OF THE GIANT BARCODES THAT DOT THE SERENGETI LANDSCAPE.

I don't know why, but in the back of my mind I have always had a sinking feeling that I stole this joke from someone. If you recognize it, drop me a line. If not, I am very proud of it.

"AFTER YOU", SAID MISS MANNERS.
"OH, YOU FIRST" INSISTED MRS. ETIQUETTE.

IN THE SCREENWRITERS GUILD, SECRETARY IS THE MOST COVETED POSITION.

"PLAY DEAD. THEY WON'T EAT ANYTHING THAT'S DEAD. NO, WAIT, THAT MIGHT BE BEARS ... IT'S FUNNY, THE THINGS YOU FORGET."

FOR YEARS HE HAD ENJOYED THE GOOD LIFE AT THE ROYAL COURT, UNTIL ONE DAY, PRINCE FREDERICK OF NORWAY POINTED OUT THAT THERE WAS, IN FACT, NO SUCH TITLE AS THE GRAND DUKE OF FUNKADELIA.

"... AND THEN SOME GIANT MACHINE PUNCHED A HOLE THROUGH MY STOMACH, AND THAT'S HOW YOU WERE BORN."

"OH GREAT, WE'LL NEVER WIN WITH THIS NERD ON OUR TEAM."

AT THE WORLD MEDITATING CHAMPIONSHIPS.

What the hell? This really, really didn't belong in the funny pages.

AND THEN, ON THE DUSTY SHORES OF THE GITCHE GUMEE, THE AGE OLD QUESTION OF WHO WOULD WIN A FIGHT BETWEEN A NARWHAL AND A WILDEBEEST WAS FINALLY ANSWERED.

Is this what a narwhal looks like? I know Google images is just a click away, but like Guy, I usually skip the research hoping whatever I come up with is funnier. This might have been one of those instances where he said, "I dare you to draw a _____ without looking it up."

"I can't escape it, Doc— that feeling that I'm stuck in some lame New Yorker cartoon."

I hate most New Yorker cartoons. But to be fair, I also hate museums and classical music.

"LOOK AT HIM OUT THERE...SO COLD, SO DISTANT. WHY DO I ALWAYS FALL FOR THE BAD BOYS?"

"THIS SUCKS. LET'S TRY AND START THE WAVE."

 After two years of rejecting the word "sucks" on account of his young children, Rodd finally relented.

See, here's another example. If I had just traced an image I found on the Internet, that space shuttle in the background would look exactly like it's supposed to instead of the simulacrum my brain came up with. I learned that word from the *New Yorker*.

THE HOUSE THAT RUTH BUILT

This guy really looks like Woody Allen.

He does? I don't think so.

"WAY TO GO, CHANG. NOT SUCH A GREAT WALL IF YOU FORGET TO LOCK THE DOOR."

THE GREAT SLINGSHOT OF MONGOLIA

SOMETIMES, WHEN THEY WERE BORED, THE GODS WOULD PLAY JENGA® WITH THE CUTE LITTLE WALL THAT THE HUMANS MADE.

MOST PEOPLE DON'T KNOW THAT THE GREAT WALL WAS ORIGINALLY BUILT OUT OF POPSICLE STICKS. OF COURSE, BACK THEN IT WAS JUST CALLED "THE WALL".

62

THE LESS CELEBRATED, BUT STILL SPECTACULAR, COMBOVER EAGLE.

THE CAKE WAS GREAT AND THE ICE CREAM WAS DELICIOUS, BUT DEEP DOWN INSIDE, HE KNEW THAT SOME DAY HIS PARENTS WOULD DISCOVER THAT "F" WASN'T FOR FANTASTIC, AND THEN NONE OF IT WOULD BE WORTH IT.

SUDDENLY, BECKY NOTICED SOMETHING WHICH GAVE HER PAUSE.

 You can learn a lot about a man from the way he draws. For instance, now I know that Rodd wears tighty whities.

63

"DANG IT, I JUST WASHED THIS STREET. BOY, EVERY TIME..."

NOW THIS BABY COMES WITH AN AUTOMATIC SUNROOF ... OR, IF YOU COME BACK AFTER 6:30, A MOONROOF.

"PSST! I HAVE NO IDEA WHAT I'M DOING."

UNBEKNOWNST TO MOST HUMANS, THE TRUE KING OF THE JUNGLE ISN'T A LION ... IT'S A CLICKING BEETLE, NAMED AL.

"AND ANOTHER THING, HE THINKS 11:11:11 IS A COOLER TIME THAN 12:34:56. I MEAN 11:11:11... COULD HE BE ANY MORE TRITE?"

 This was an actual conversation I had with a girlfriend in college. I realize now she was right. 12:34:56 is way cooler.

BUZZ WAS AMAZED BY THE INCREDIBLE SIGHT BEFORE HIM...SOMEHOW, NEIL HAD MANAGED TO WRITE HIS NAME IN THE CONDENSATION.

UHH... SORRY LINCOLN, THIS TABLE IS FOR EQUIPMENT MANAGERS FOR THE SPORTS TEAMS. I DON'T THINK CHEERLEADING COUNTS AS A SPORT .... YEESH, WHAT A NERD.

"I DIDN'T WANT TO BE ONE OF THOSE CRAZY OLD LADIES LIVING WITH A BUNCH OF CATS ... SO I GOT A BIRD TOO."

WHILE DOING ROUTINE RECON OVER THE PACIFIC OCEAN, LIEUTENANTS CROMWELL AND OLSEN MAKE A STARTLING DISCOVERY.

"OH JEEZ, I GOTTA BE THE SINGLE UNLUCKIEST GUY IN THE ENTIRE WORLD."

Those swastikas aren't part of some hidden message; there really were swastikas on the tail fins of the *Hindenburg*. Which blew me away when I looked it up on the Inter . . . er, drew upon my memory of the actual event. It also makes you wonder why, if we had a balloon full of Nazis in New Jersey, we didn't do something about it ourselves instead of letting science take its course.

"MERLE, DO YOU THINK WE SOUND STUPID WHEN WE SAY 'AARGH'? I MEAN, IT'S NOT REALLY A WORD, IS IT?"

LARRY FROZE, UNSURE OF WHAT TO DO. YES, HE WAS A DOCTOR, BUT ON THE OTHER HAND, THIS WASN'T TECHNICALLY A HOUSE.

 Everyone who specializes in some really obscure field must feel this way at some point.

Um . . . my dad told me this comic hit a little too close to home. He's a corrosion engineer. Kind of an expert on rust.

Our old boss was Mike Greenfeld, and we called him Greenie. That's where I got this idea from.

"BY THE WAY, I USUALLY SNEEZE IN TWOS. SO THAT'S ANOTHER INTERESTING THING ABOUT ME."

"MAY I PRESENT SIR ISAAC NEWTON. HE CLAIMS TO HAVE DISCOVERED SOMETHING BIG."

IT WAS A MONDAY WHEN HE DISCOVERED THE CAVE OF BAD PUNS. BY FRIDAY, HE WAS THE MOST SUCCESSFUL CARTOONIST IN HISTORY.

Stephan Pastis, who does the comic strip *Pearls Before Swine*, called the day this came out because he was sure it was about him. I had to convince him it wasn't. It was.

Which is why you followed it up with the brilliant "trim reaper" gag two days later?

DATING...THE FINAL FRONTIER. ERIC'S LOG, STARDATE: FRIDAY NIGHT.

HE'S NARRATING IT, I JUST KNOW IT. OH MAN, THIS IS SO CREEPY.

BARSOOM OR BUST

THE TRIM REAPER

"ALL I'M SAYING IS, YOU KNOW I MADE THAT
SANDWICH FOR MYSELF... I JUST THINK
SOME THINGS ARE SACRED, EARL."

OH GREAT, NOW
WE'RE ACCOMPLICES.

MOST PEOPLE DON'T KNOW THAT
TUG-O-WAR GOT ITS START IN THE LATE
1600'S WHEN, FOR A BRIEF PERIOD OF TIME,
ROPE WAS CONSIDERED LEGAL TENDER.

Is this really what people wore in the 1600s? I think it's more an
assortment of costumes from the "can't be bothered to look it up"
theatrical company: three pirates, two bankers, and Nellie Olsen from
Little House on the Prairie.

VENTURA COUNTY
PUBLIC
LIBRARY

OH, THIS WAS
NO ACCIDENT.

We have been kicked out of a lot of papers, but never with more venom
than by the editor of the *Ventura County Star.*

"WOULD YOU MIND HOLDING MY HAND, JIM? THE TRUTH IS, I'M DEATHLY AFRAID OF FLYING."

I'M AN ARTISTIC GENIUS. I BET NO ONE HAS EVER PAINTED A PLAIN OLD BOWL OF FRUIT BEFORE.

NAH, IT'S ALWAYS BEEN A POT OF GRUEL. I'M NOT EVEN SURE WHERE THAT GOLD RUMOR CAME FROM. ANYWAYS...ENJOY!

 Every time we use it, we know "anyways" is incorrect, but keep those e-mails coming anyways.

My friend Adam Nathanson's dad gave us all the medical terms, but he still won't give me drugs.

 Rodd was so embarrassed by this "joke" that he drew an extra panel to publicly make fun of me. Looking back, I don't blame him.

HIS NAME WAS ACTUALLY LARRY, BUT BY THE TIME SHE STARTED GUESSING RANDOM NONSENSE LIKE "RUMPELSTILTSKIN" HE GOT BORED AND TOLD HER SHE WAS RIGHT.

AT THE CHINESE FINGERCUFF FACTORY

THAT NIGHT, NEIL THOMAS DECLARED HIMSELF THE POET LAUREATE OF 1673 SHEFFIELD LANE.

 That's my dad's real name and old address. I was hoping he would get annoying mail from it, but he didn't.

BECAUSE IT CONTAINS THOUSANDS OF INDIVIDUAL CHARACTERS, BURPING THE ALPHABET IN JAPAN IS TRULY A GLORIOUS ACHIEVEMENT.

TWO DAYS AGO, DECEMBER 6th, WAS A DAY WHICH WILL LIVE IN FAMY, BUT YESTERDAY... NO SIR.

Snowy!

...AND THEN THE PRINCE TOOK THE GLASS SLIPPER THROUGHOUT THE KINGDOM, WHERE HE DISCOVERED THAT IT FIT 1,184 DAMSELS, OR ROUGHLY 4.8 PERCENT OF THE POPULACE.

 I have always wondered about this. There are only so many shoe sizes. Unless Cinderella was a total freak, that slipper had to fit lots of women. Or, possibly, it's just a fairy tale.

The alternate caption for this read: "I am the great warrior Achilles. Tremble before me, for I have but one secret vulnerability, and no one ever guesses the heel. Oh crud." Hmm. Maybe neither one is funny.

AS IT TURNS OUT, DANGER DOESN'T COME IN ALL SHAPES AND SIZES...THE EXCEPTIONS BEING THE DODECAGON AND 3 FEET 7 INCHES.

 I don't know.

"I'M THINKING SOMETHING A LITTLE MORE MODEST... SAY, WHATEVER 1,000 SLAVES CAN DO IN 50 YEARS."

AND WITH THAT, THE SIMPLE MALAISE THAT HAD BEEN BUBBLING UP FOR MONTHS OFFICIALLY BECAME A GENERAL MALAISE.

SUDDENLY, GOD WONDERED IF SAINT ANDREW HAD A COOLER CELL PHONE THAN HIM.

MOST PEOPLE DON'T KNOW THAT
IN ADDITION TO THE THEORY OF RELATIVITY,
EINSTEIN WAS ALSO THE INVENTOR OF
THE "KNEEL AND PUSH".

I don't know why she's wearing an apron. Rodd?

To hide her genitals. Duh. Didn't you learn anything from the cat/dog comic?

"SOLOMON, WHAT DID I TELL YOU ABOUT GIVING
THE CHALK OUTLINES THOUGHT BUBBLES!?"

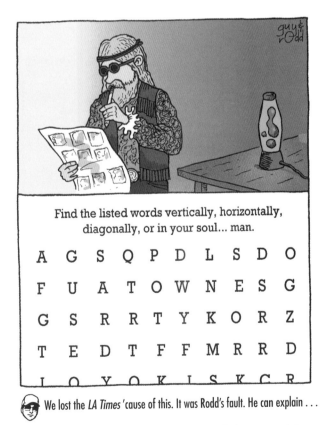

Find the listed words vertically, horizontally, diagonally, or in your soul... man.

A G S Q P D L S D O
F U A T O W N E S G
G S R R T Y K O R Z
T E D T F F M R R D
L O Y O K I S K C R

We lost the *LA Times* 'cause of this. It was Rodd's fault. He can explain . . .

I erroneously thought hippies used LSD and smoked pot, so I might have hidden those words in the word search for historical accuracy. I also hid the names of my three ungrateful sons in there, so that might have ruffled some feathers too. (My youngest is named Pot, after the dictator.)

The original comic had them in bed smoking a cigarette. So there, *LA Times*, we do have scruples.

"SO THERE I WAS CARRYING OVER 100 TIMES MY OWN BODY WEIGHT... YOU KNOW WHAT THAT'S LIKE, RIGHT... WHEN YOU CAN CARRY OVER 100 TIMES YOUR OWN BODY WEIGHT?"

"MY ONLY REGRET, IS THAT I WON'T LIVE TO SEE THE MOVIE".

AND THEN, ON A BEAUTIFUL SPRING DAY IN 2003, WITH THE SCENT OF RHODODENDRUMS FILLING THE AIR, ADAM HINDS BECAME THE FIRST, AND STILL ONLY, PERSON TO ACTUALLY USE ZAPF DINGBATS.

 Honestly, what the fark is that font for? Anyone?

HOUSED DEEP WITHIN THE BOWELS OF THE MOTION PICTURE ASSOCIATION OF AMERICA IS A MAN NAMED WALLACE McENTYRE, AND HE, AND HE ALONE, UNDERSTANDS WHAT MAY AND MAY NOT BE APPROPRIATE FOR CHILDREN UNDER THIRTEEN.

"ABRAMOWITZ AND LOWENSTEIN, YOU'VE CERTAINLY EARNED THIS, BUT UNFORTUNATELY WE DON'T HAVE ENOUGH ROOM ON THE LETTERHEAD... SMITH, CONGRATULATIONS!"

EVERYONE'S HEARD OF THE STAIRWAY TO HEAVEN, BUT MOST PEOPLE DON'T KNOW IT WAS ACTUALLY BUILT TO KEEP THE FATTIES OUT.

 This one, as expected, generated a lot of hate mail. I can't say I blame the people who were offended, but I still think it's a funny comic.

"I'M AN HERBOLOGIST... I STUDY THIS GUY".

 Tracksuit! (It's a drinking game.)

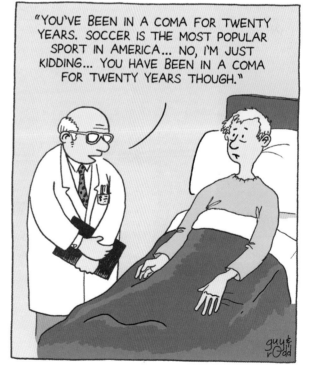

"YOU'VE BEEN IN A COMA FOR TWENTY YEARS. SOCCER IS THE MOST POPULAR SPORT IN AMERICA... NO, I'M JUST KIDDING... YOU HAVE BEEN IN A COMA FOR TWENTY YEARS THOUGH."

CAPTAIN ICICLE WAS SITTING NEXT TO DOCTOR MAGMA, AND MS. AQUAMAN SWORE THIS WOULD BE THE LAST TIME HER HUSBAND HANDLED THE SEATING ARRANGEMENTS.

A CONNECTICUT YANKEE IN KING ARTHUR'S BATHROOM

"I WANT TO KNOW EVERYTHING ABOUT YOU, UNLESS IT'S BORING, AND THEN FOR GOD'S SAKE SPARE ME".

This has bugged me since I was a kid. They might as well just claim he's awesome at taking the elevator.

 I considered lots of nerd icons, but at the end of the day, Famke Janssen is a really funny name.

And once again, the concept of brevity takes a hit.

NEVER BEFORE SEEN OUTTAKES FROM THE SPINNING SCENE IN "THE SOUND OF MUSIC".

When we are super rich . . . next year . . . we will buy a vineyard and market a wine called "Best Blue."

Yes, you guessed it. This is Guy and my fantasy of how we'll end up together in life.

All my gay friends tell me the guy on the right looks way more gay.

SOUP WAS ALWAYS DIFFICULT AT URI'S HOUSE.

I think they are especially jealous that the gardener is a hot chick in a bikini.

ROBERTO PAUSED TO ADMIRE HIS WORK.
NEVER BEFORE HAD HE PLASTERED
A CEILING SO BEAUTIFULLY.
MINUTES LATER, A YOUNG PUNK NAMED
MICHELANGELO WOULD RUIN EVERYTHING.

 This guy was bitter for the rest of his life.

"SOME OF THESE TREES HAVE BEEN HERE FOR
2000 YEARS... AND THEY STILL CAN'T TALK
...MAN, WE'RE AWESOME!"

ONE LAST TIME MR. GALLAGHER,
"WHAT HAPPENS IN VEGAS STAYS IN VEGAS"
IS NOT, NOR WILL IT EVER BE,
AN ACCEPTABLE LEGAL PRECEDENT.

"OOH WATCH YOUR STEP, THAT'S MY NOBEL
PRIZE. I WONDER HOW IT GOT DOWN THERE,
CRAZY NOBEL PRIZE...........NOBEL PRIZE".

 Not sure why Jebediah doesn't just look out the window.

Then he'd be watching, not listening. This is the only drawing I've altered after the fact, because the original had the string all loose and lying on the ground, until a reader pointed out that it has to be pulled tight to work.

WELL YEAH, I GUESS ON SOME LEVEL I KNEW IT WOULD LOOK HILARIOUS, BUT MOSTLY IT'S JUST BECAUSE WE'RE POOR.

"SO I HEAR INFLATION IS REALLY RUNNING RAMPANT. SHOULDN'T BE A PROBLEM THOUGH, RIGHT PENNY? COUGH! -- OBSOLETE -- COUGH!"

I think it's funny that all the American coins shown here actually face left while Lincoln faces right.

BEFORE THEY SETTLED ON "ACTION", MANY DIRECTORS WOULD START A TAKE WITH "GENTLEMEN, LET US COMMENCE WITH OUR FILMMAKERLY DUTIES, TUT-TUT".

"HEY I GOT ANOTHER ROLL OF THOUSANDS,
THAT'S THE THIRD TIME THIS WEEK...
SO WHAT'D YOU GET?"

 Go Mets!!!!!!

"I DARE SAY,
I DON'T LIKE
WHERE THIS
IS GOING".

NOW WHEN POLISHED THIS MAY TURN OUT
TO BE A GEM OF SOME SIGNIFICANCE...
OR IT MAY JUST BE A ROCK.
WHAT'S EXCITING, I THINK, IS NOT KNOWING.
SO WHAT DO YOU SAY BABY?

SEVEN, THAT'S YOUR LUCKY NUMBER!?
BOY, I REALLY THOUGHT IT WOULD BE SOME
SORT OF FRACTION, OR AN INTEGER THAT
CAN ONLY BE EXPRESSED ON THE MOON,
OR I DON'T KNOW... SOMETHING.
I MEAN, SEVEN!?

All these numbers are freeways in LA. Of course by the time this comic ran, we'd already been kicked out of the *LA Times* (see page 82).

MONSTER CHARIOT RACES

SANDRO FAILED TO ANTICIPATE THE
SERIOUSNESS OF THE OLYMPICS.

Our editor thought the name Ahmed was stereotypical and asked us to change it. Our editor really didn't get this joke at all.

GRANDPA WAS PROUD OF THE EFFECT HIS SIGNATURE STOLEN NOSE TRICK WAS HAVING ON THE YOUNG CROWD. IT WASN'T UNTIL LATER THAT ANYONE EXPLAINED TO HIM HOW DYLAN HAD LOST HIS REAL NOSE IN A HORRIBLE SLEDDING ACCIDENT.

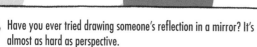
Have you ever tried drawing someone's reflection in a mirror? It's almost as hard as perspective.

SHE HAD ALWAYS HAD A THING FOR REBELS.

HERE'S LOOKING AT YOU, KID.

I REALLY THINK I COULD HAVE LOVED YOU... IF ONLY YOU COULD TALK LIKE A NORMAL PERSON.

"I HAVE A FEELING WE'RE NOT IN KANSAS ANYMORE".

 I always thought the quote was "Something tells me we're not in Kansas anymore." The joke would have been better if it was.

 Have you ever looked at those things? They are made out of cardboard and motel carpet, but they cost more than kidneys.

We hoped this one would get picked up by a bunch of angry bloggers, but it didn't. Nerds.

 Smoking in bed is dangerous.

BILL IS THE MOST REBELLIOUS HELL'S ANGEL OF THEM ALL.

THANK GOD I FINALLY CAUGHT UP WITH YOU... I JUST WANT TO ASK, WHAT THE HECK DOES "MEEP MEEP" MEAN? I MEAN "MEEP" ISN'T A WORD IS IT?

I'VE ACTUALLY ALWAYS HATED GRAPES, BUT YOU KNOW, IMAGE IS EVERYTHING.

That girl is totally smooshing that daisy into that guy's fingernail. I don't know what it means, but it seems filthy.

"I THREW AWAY THE LOVE SEAT, ARNOLD... IT JUST FELT DISHONEST".

ANNUAL MEETING
GARFUNKEL IS BETTER SOCIETY

HAVING NEGLECTED TO PAY HIS GAS BILL, HIROKI INADVERTENTLY LAUNCHES A CULINARY REVOLUTION.

"UH, YEAH, IT'S SUPPOSED TO BE LIKE THAT... IT'S A... IT'S A NEW INVENTION".

Hang in there!

Hang in there!

Hang in there!

"IT'S ONE OF THE MOST SUCCESSFUL MOTIVATIONAL POSTERS OF ALL TIME, OR WHATEVER... I DON'T LIKE TO MAKE A BIG DEAL OUT OF IT... TOP FIVE IF YOU HAVE TO KNOW".

COULDN'T YOU AT LEAST **PRETEND** TO HAVE A PROBLEM?

SHRINKS IN HEAVEN

JOE BOB EDISON, STANDING NEXT TO HIS GREATEST INVENTION.

I ACTUALLY HAD THE ELVES PUT TOGETHER SOME HEADLIGHTS, SO NOW YOU CAN GO BACK TO, WELL, YOU KNOW... BEING A FREAK.

"THAT'S JEB LAMBERT. HE WAS ACTUALLY THE FIRST ONE TO SAY 'PAPER OR PLASTIC'. BEFORE THAT EVERYONE SAID 'PLASTIC OR PAPER'... I MEAN, CAN YOU IMAGINE?"

Always be wary of ordering the fresh fish in a restaurant that also calls its pepper fresh.

This one took an unusually long time to draw, and I drew it a year in advance. It was supposed to be a parody of one of those illustrated Sunday school morality tales, but I'm actually proud of how it came out, and it might get me a gig doing children's books someday.

In LA we have a 99-cent store directly across from a 98-cent store. I always wonder if the shoppers at the 99-cent store look down their nose at the ones across the street.

THE NURSE HELD UP A BEAUTIFUL BABY KNORK... NEEDLESS TO SAY, THE SPOON WAS DEVASTATED.

 The Whisper Lounge is a restaurant where Rodd and I used to have lunch to go over comics. That's Kimmi, our favorite waitress.

115

CHINESE SCRABBLE

I don't know what this joke is saying about the Chinese language, but it's probably offensive.

LATER IN LIFE, GANDALF WOULD BECOME THE GREATEST CROSSING GUARD IN MARICOPA COUNTY HISTORY.

Rodd worked on the trailers for the *Lord of the Rings* franchise.

 This is a recurring theme in *The Family Circus* . . . you know, kids throwing themselves to their death.

 The original comic had God's son standing there with a baseball glove, but you can't joke about Jesus like that in most newspapers.

IT IS A LESSER KNOWN HISTORICAL FACT THAT SIR EDMUND HILLARY WAS ALSO THE FIRST PERSON TO CLIMB MOUNT EVEREST AND FORGET TO TAKE THE LENS CAP OFF.

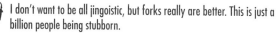
I don't want to be all jingoistic, but forks really are better. This is just a billion people being stubborn.

 When you were a kid, that credit sequence was the height of special effects.

BECAUSE SHE'D ALWAYS HAD A CRUSH ON THE HANDSOME BUT STUPID PROFESSOR, SOMETIMES AT NIGHT SHE'D FIX SOME OF HIS MORE OBVIOUS COMPUTATIONAL ERRORS.

"PSST! I JUST REALIZED SOMETHING... I'M HELLA BORED".

 Someone wrote to tell us that the complete and utter nuclear destruction of the world isn't funny . . . oh, thanks for clearing that up.

AND THAT WAS THE LAST TIME LANCE WAS ALLOWED TO LEAD THE FLOCK.

EXPRESS LANE
10 ITEMS OR LESS

SORRY MA'AM, BUT A RULE IS A RULE.

CHK CHK!

We had no idea we'd stepped into the most divisive issue of our time: whether checkout signs should actually say "Ten items or *fewer*."

AT THE END OF THE DAY, ALL JOHN HENRY BARNSBY WAS GUILTY OF WAS TAKING A LIE DETECTOR TEST DURING THE GREAT SAN FRANCISCO EARTHQUAKE OF 1906.

OH, SO THAT'S WHERE I PUT MY BEAR.

THE FIRST THING YOU SHOULD KNOW IS THAT IF I TIE A SCARF TO THE DOORKNOB, THAT MEANS IT'S COLD OUTSIDE, AND YOU SHOULD PROBABLY WEAR A SCARF.

 Go Wesleyan!!!!!

EVERYBODY MADE FUN OF JOSH FOR BEING AFRAID OF HIS SHADOW, BUT LATER THAT DAY, THEY WOULD ALL BE SORRY.

I'M SORRY I SAID YOUR HAIR WAS STUPID... I WAS JUST UPSET ABOUT LOSING.

THE APPRENTIC

Of course, even if he had the sword, he would still be grossly outnumbered and dead.

BECAUSE HE HAD DONE SOME SHADY THINGS IN LIFE, ASHTON WAS SURPRISED BY THE WARM RECEPTION HE RECEIVED IN HEAVEN. THEN JESUS POPPED OUT AND YELLED "PUNK'D"!

We're actually terrible at depicting planes the way they really park at terminals, which is perpendicular.

SUPERHEROES AND THEIR WEAKNESSES

NO ADAM, "AWESOME" IS NOT AN ACCEPTABLE CHOICE OF WHAT YOU WANT TO BE WHEN YOU GROW UP.

Scratch-'n-win!

A donation has been made in your name to the National Earth Day fund.

 This should actually read "uninterested" as several lawyers pointed out.

These guys just tied for last place.

This is the cover of our second book, but, of course, you already know that . . .

"WE'VE ISOLATED THE OBESITY GENE DOWN TO ONE OF THESE TWO".

"OH MAN, HE JUST NAILED THAT TRIPLE ENTENDRE... THAT ALL BUT GUARANTEES HIM A MEDAL".

 A lot of people thought we were slandering Judaism in this one. But, you see . . . oh, figure it out for yourself.

CONFUCIUS SAY: SHUT UP.

You almost never see words like "extermination" on two lines in real life.

ACCORDING TO INDUSTRY NEWSLETTERS, KETCHUP REMAIN'S THE WORLD'S MOST POPULAR CONDIMENT. MUSTARD CONTINUES TO BE PRETTY LAME, AND SORTA JEALOUS.

IT WOULD HAVE PLACED HIM ALONGSIDE SUCH GREATS AS DAVINCI AND VAN GOGH, BUT THEN, ON A WHIM, HE DECIDED TO ADD SOME STINK LINES.

INTERNATIONAL SYMBOLS

EVERYTHING'S A-OK.

DO YOU WANT A DRINK?

THERE IS A MEDIUM SIZED SEA OTTER ATTACKING MY KNEE.

A teacher in Florida sent us an article about a real incident where a student was attacked by an otter. She couldn't believe this was a coincidence.

P.S. Do *not* use the symbol for "A-OK" when traveling abroad, especially in Italy. Apparently it isn't truly an international symbol.

AND THEN, RIGHT IN THE MIDDLE OF A WARRANT/WINGER DOUBLE BILL, ROB MYERS BECOMES THE FIRST PERSON IN HISTORY TO ACTUALLY HAVE HIS SOCKS ROCKED OFF.

Rob Myers is a friend of mine who is a total music snob. He would never be caught dead at a Warrant concert . . . although he does love Winger.

EXCUSE ME, COULD EVERYONE BE QUIET, I'M TRYING TO TALK ON MY CELL PHONE.

SUDDENLY, ROARK REALIZED WHAT HAD BEEN BUGGING HIM FOR THE LAST 18 MONTHS.

THE OMNICOM CORPORATION

HEY MISTER, WHERE'S THE DOOR?

The parent company of the company I work for is named Omnicom. I tease them that it sounds like a made-up name for comics, like "Globo-Tech."

"YOU KNOW, JUST BECAUSE THEY ASK, DOESN'T MEAN YOU HAVE TO LET THEM FLY".

EVERYONE ALWAYS THOUGHT M. C. ESCHER
HAD AN INCREDIBLE IMAGINATION,
BUT REALLY HE JUST
GREW UP IN A WEIRD HOUSE.

 I've never actually worn Dockers. Possibly they are great.

 Maria is actually Rob Myers's better half. She always says the word "actually." Actually.

WELL, WE JUST BECAME UNSPECTACULAR.

Anyone who has detailed knowledge of the Wright brothers' first flight knows I've drawn their plane backward. I think I'll keep it this way for all future printings, because it seems like it would have been more aerodynamic this way.

SIX MONTHS LATER THEY WOULD BE SHARING THE NOBEL PRIZE, BUT FOR NOW ALL THEY COULD DO WAS STARE IN AMAZEMENT AT WHAT THEY HAD DISCOVERED... TWO INCREDIBLY WELL PRESERVED SPECIMENS FROM THE STYROFOAM AGE.

THAT'S ACTUALLY A COMMON MISCONCEPTION. THE TRUTH IS WE CAN GO EIGHT DAYS WITHOUT WATER, BUT ONLY IF WE DRINK A LOT OF OTHER STUFF... YOU KNOW, LIKE APPLE JUICE.

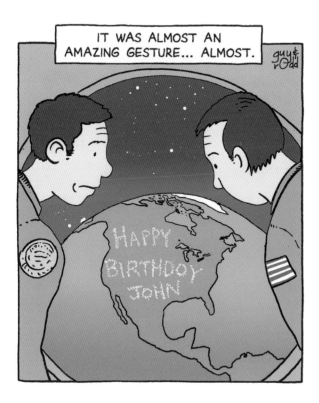

IT WAS ALMOST AN AMAZING GESTURE... ALMOST.

HAPPY BIRTHDAY JOHN

STEVE WAS INNOCENTLY PLAYING WITH
HIS FLAGS WHEN, ALL OF A SUDDEN,
SOMETHING TERRIBLE HAPPENED.

BEFORE THE SPIDER INCIDENT, PETER PARKER WAS BRIEFLY IMBUED WITH THE INCREDIBLE POWERS OF THE WORM.

HEY LOOKEE HERE, THIS IS QUITE A... UH... SHOOT, WHAT DO YOU CALL IT WHEN A BUNCH OF US GET TOGETHER?

HERE I AM BEING BORN. HERE I AM SHOWING YOU THIS PICTURE. AND NOW, IF YOU'LL EXCUSE ME, I HAVE TO DIE.

FRUIT FLY PHOTO ALBUMS

I've told Guy it's actually mayflies that live for one day, but he still keeps feeding me fruit fly gags.

...AND **THIS** LITTLE PIGGIE STAYED HOME...

MY GOD, HE'S INSANE.

What psycho came up with this?

 Our next book is going to be nothing but Kruschev comics.

WHEN VEGETARIANS DREAM

We got a lot of angry letters from vegetarians who insist they don't dream of meat. (A) It's a comic. (B) I'm a vegetarian, and I would eat the heck out of a steak if it grew in a field.

 People in the olden days were ugly.

IN CHINA, ALPHABET SOUP CAN BE A CHOKING HAZARD.

 Again, Guy makes a brutal attack on Chinese culture.

ALL THE DEMONS CHIPPED IN TO GET SATAN A GAG GIFT FOR HIS BIRTHDAY.

THE PARROT WAS PROUD TO HAVE MASTERED THE HUMAN TONGUE... NEVER SUSPECTING THAT HE ACTUALLY LIVED WITH IDIOTS.

ROO ROO!

ROO ROO!

ROO ROO!

ROO ROO!

 "Roo roo" is a term Gene Weingarten uses on a regular basis in his *Washington Post* online chat. We have no idea what it means.

ANOTHER NEAT TRICK IS TO CUT REGULAR SPAGHETTI INTO LITTLE PIECES, AND NEXT THING YOU KNOW YOU'VE GOT YOURSELF A BOWL OF SPAGHETTI-I-S.

Dear Guy & Rodd:
I read the comic page a lot and I don't find yours to be funny. I have a few suggestions for it. Feel free to use any you want.

1. make a guy kick a donkey in the face.

2. Make a kid fall off of a moving car.

3. Make a human kill an alien.

PEANUT BUTTER

Well, those are my ideas. Please tell me when they will be in the paper.

David Singh
San Francisco, CA

Dear David:
Now. guy & rOdd

This was a real letter we turned into a comic, but our lawyer (OK, it was Stephan Pastis) advised us against using the reader's name, so I used the name of a client of mine. I don't think he was happy we used his name, and I know the real reader was unhappy we didn't use his. The real letter was from Gavin Whitaker in Draper, Utah.

I'M HAPPY YOU'RE A REAL BOY NOW, PINNOCHIO... THE THING IS, I ONLY LIKE GUYS WITH HUGE NOSES.

guy & rOdd

I DON'T KNOW HOW TO BREAK THIS TO YOU, BUT THE WORLD GOT TOGETHER AND DECIDED THAT FROM NOW ON, EVERYONE IS ENTITLED TO HIS OPINION... EXCEPT YOU.

guy & rOdd

 This is when I was working on the campaign for *An Inconvenient Truth*.

 This was opening day.

 I am sure flowers feel this way.

Do people hold hands in these groups? If so, count me out.

ONCE AGAIN, THE CONVERSATION GETS TOO HEATED, AND THE SELECTION OF A STATE MUFFIN HAS TO BE SHELVED UNTIL NEXT YEAR.

HISTORY HAS MERCIFULLY FORGOTTEN THE INCREDIBLY BRIEF REIGN OF DINGUS KHAN.

Lots of churches have asked to use this in their newsletters. Hopefully that makes up for some of the horrible things Rodd has done (see pages 31, 82, etc.).

SHORTLY THEREAFTER, THEY WOULD MAKE SWEEPING CHANGES TO THEIR POLICIES.

SECRETLY SHE'D ALWAYS HATED YOUNG ADAM KASSAN.

 Hopefully this book is in color.

 One day we are going to get sued, but we will win 'cause this comic is based on fact.

THE INVISIBLE MAN LOVED TO
MESS WITH WONDER WOMAN.

AND NOW A MOMENT OF SILENCE SO THAT
WE MAY NEVER FORGET THE TRAGIC EVENTS
OF MARCH 31ST... WHEN WE RAN OUT OF
NAPKINS ON SLOPPY JOE DAY.

PALMS JR. HIGH

LET IT GO, NEIL!

McGOVERN 4 PREZ

MINUTES LATER THE COURSE OF COMEDY
WOULD BE CHANGED FOREVER.

DING DONG...
who's there?

KNOCK KNOCK...
(may I help you?

TAP, TAP, TAP...
hello, and how may I be
of assistance to you?

We're pretty sure Michael Bay stole this joke for *Transformers*.

I wish we wouldn't have put a caption on this. It's totally unnecessary, right?

PREHISTORIC PIRATES

SORRY, ARE YOU ON THE LIST?

AND THAT'S HOW PALESTINE BECAME THE FIRST NATION TO DEFEAT THE MONGOLS.

MMMMXLVIII ANIMAL OLYMPICS

WHAT DO YOU SAY NEXT YEAR WE HAVE SOME NON CHEETAH RACES?

LISTEN, I'M SURE JANITORIAL WORK IS FASCINATING, AND IT'S A VERY GENEROUS OFFER... IT'S JUST THAT WE'RE PRETTY SELECTIVE ABOUT WHOSE PAPERS WE ARCHIVE HERE AT HARVARD.

BEFORE THEY AGREED ON "THE STAR SPANGLED BANNER", THERE WAS A BRIEF PERIOD WHEN AMERICA WOULD CELEBRATE ITS PRIDE WITH A ROUSING RENDITION OF WRECKX-N-EFFECT'S "RUMPSHAKER".

WAIT, ARE YOU ALLERGIC TO BEES OR NUTS?... I CAN NEVER REMEMBER

NOW TO THE LAYPERSON THIS MAY SEEM LIKE JUST A JUNKY LITTLE HOUSE, BUT IT'S ACTUALLY A REALLY NICE TREEHOUSE... CONVENIENTLY LOCATED ON THE GROUND.

HE SMILED TO HIMSELF, ENJOYING HIS VICTORY IN HIDE AND SEEK.

BUT SOON, THE NEXT ACTIVITY WOULD START.

 Just now, trying to think of something to write about this comic, I realized the ticket has the caption from the bird comic on the previous page. Weird. Or lazy. Or both. Rodd?

 I don't know, man; you write the captions.

IT WAS ORIGINALLY GOING TO BE CALLED THE "ST. LOUIS M", BUT HALFWAY THROUGH CONSTRUCTION, EVERYONE KIND OF DECIDED THEY'D JUST HAD ENOUGH.

BEFORE COOKIES BECAME THE NORM, SOME CHINESE RESTAURANTS EXPERIMENTED WITH "FORTUNE KUNG PAO BROCCOLIS".

OH, I'M NOT ACTUALLY THE MASCOT... JUST INSANE.

 That batter is standing on home plate, which means the pitcher is allowed to hit him. Rodd is from Australia.

HE WATCHED IN AWE AS THE YOUNG MAN CROSSED HIS PATH, AND HE THOUGHT TO HIMSELF, "MAN, BASEBALL HATS ARE COOL"!

IT WAS A LAST MINUTE CHANGE, BUT A GOOD ONE.

WAR & PEACE & CABBAGE

 This would probably be better without a caption too.

I drew this after reading a bunch of Dan Clowes comics and feeling like a totally inferior artist.

Seriously, why doesn't he do this? You know he wants to, and then he ends up choosing Hitler or Kenneth Starr and it kills him.

 This should be brussels sprout, but it looked weird.

 I don't think *Shrek the Third* would have done nearly as well if it hadn't made an appearance in our comic.

I think about ten million people started doing this. I wonder if anyone actually finished.

 This comic is so lame. I can't believe it's the last one in the book. Go back and read page 1 real quick before you put this down.

In the Beginning . . .

We'd like to say the drawings included in this section prove that Guy and Rodd had dreams of a career in comics since kindergarten. But the sad truth is they were drawn by Guy when he was twenty-five-years-old. Rodd found them in his office, and from there the dream was born: what if we took these horrible drawings with mediocre jokes and replaced them with mediocre drawings?

Please enjoy this brief look back at the painful contractions leading up to the birth of *Brevity*.

Before Birds and Bees.

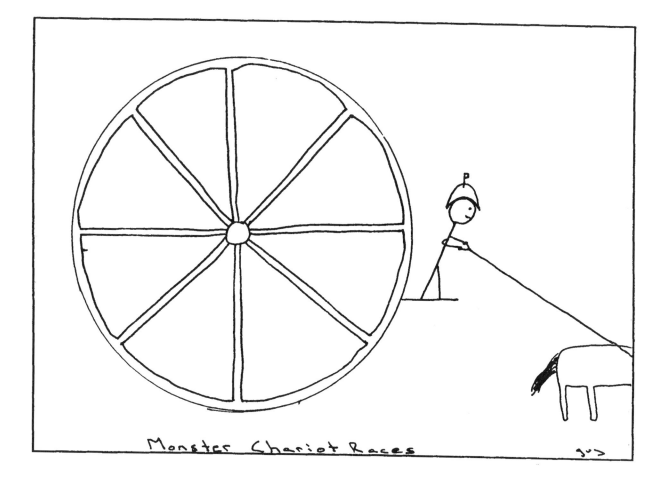

Monster Chariot Races

Jesus Saves

Old West Proms

First the hotdog-on-a-stick man noticed it. Then the performers, because they are sensitive to such things... There was tension on the midway.